SPEECH

OF THE

HON. EDWARDS PIERREPONT,

DELIVERED BEFORE

The Republican Mass Meeting, at Cooper Institute,

September 25, 1872.

NEW YORK:

EVENING POST STEAM PRESSES, 41 NASSAU STREET, CORNER LIBERTY.

1872.

Fellow Citizens :—I have not come to defend Gen. Grant. I point you to the record he has made, which is eternal; in the blaze of whose increasing splendor foul slanders will shrivel as a scroll, and base revilers perish as stubble.

Nor have I come to defame Horace Greeley. The good which he has done will live after him; the evil—let it be interred with his old clothes and his vain and foolish aspirations for the presidency.

I have come to talk with you on public affairs, that we may reason together, and see what is, on the whole, best in this epoch of our history.

A great nation, about to commit its destinies for years to the guidance of one man, will pause and consider well before it casts its vote.

When the deed is done, regrets, however deep and sincere, will not avail. Let us look fairly at this question of the candidates, and see which, under all the circumstances, ought to receive your suffrage.

A few months ago Horace Greeley published to the world his views of the Democratic Party in these words:

"It is rebel at the core to-day—hardly able to reconcile the defeats of Lee, Johnston, Bragg, Hood and Price, and the consequent downfall of its beloved Confederacy, with its traditional faith in Divine Providence. It would hail the election of a Democratic President in 1872 as a virtual reversal of the Appomattox surrender. It would come into power with the hate, the chagrin, the wrath, the mortification of ten bitter years to impel and guide its steps. It would devote itself to taking off or reducing tax after tax, until the Treasury was deprived of the means of paying interest on the national debt, and would hail the tidings of national bankruptcy with unalloyed gladness and unconcealed exultation. Whatever chastisement may be deserved for our national sins, we must hope that this disgrace and humiliation will be spared us."

Mr. Greeley has uttered many brave words in the cause of truth, but none more true than these.

A northern doughface, slopping over with the lukewarm milk of human kindness, may believe that the late rebels are sorry, repentant and honestly accept the situation with intent to abide by it. But no man with an intellect above good-natured idiocy, at all informed of the past conduct and present sentiment of the late Confederates, can doubt that they mean to gain by intrigue what they lost by war; that to a man they are sorry that they failed in their wicked plot to subvert the Government, and that they would to-day dig a deeper chasm and fill it full with blood, if they did not fear that brave patriots from the North, seizing their old guns, would row over it.

Fellow-citizens, let me read a page of our past history. As early as 1818 the South proposed to allow the Territory of Missouri to become a State. The North opposed this proposition unless slavery were excluded. Maine was not then admitted to the Union, and the advocates of slavery were determined that Maine should not be admitted without slavery unless Missouri was at the same time admitted with it. In 1820 a compromise was effected, and the bill which allowed Missouri to come in with slavery provided that human bondage should forever thereafter be excluded from all territory north of the parallel 36° 30′, which was the southern boundary of Missouri. This solemn compact, which the trusting North believed to be "forever," as it expressly promised, was trampled down in 1854, at the behest of the South, and then, for the first time, the North awoke to the fact that slaveholders kept no faith, but, corrupting one Northern man after another, by seductive promises of the Presidency, they grew emboldened and threw off disguises, violated every pledge, and trampled down justice and humanity, with shameless perfidy, repealed the sacred compact, and set up the hellish fiend of slavery to be a worshiped god throughout this land of freedom!

But that was not enough. The worshipers of this demon saw that martyr-fires were burning in the North, and that from their ashes dangerous converts to freedom were springing fast, and the devotees of the "peculiar institution" plotted the overthrow of our government to preserve this great abomination. Democratic Conventions, the Peace Congress, Union-saving speeches of timid old politicians, the prostration of

Northern divines, citing texts from Holy Writ, and trying with Heaven's livery to conceal their devil-worship, were all of no avail. The Union must be rent, the old flag insulted, and war, with its unnumbered woes, must come. You know the rest. Weeks, months and years passed on in war. Save to the eye of faith and to the heart trusting in a righteous God, success seemed doubtful. Mr. Greeley wanted to let the rebels go; and now, in turn, the rebels want to make Mr. Greeley President of the United States.

In those dark days, when our generals, one after another, failed, there was *one who did not fail.* He took the sword of Lee, and the accursed rebellion writhed over and seemed to die. There is some life yet in its rotting remains, and it will show lively signs if Mr. Greeley is elected. And hence you see why the late Governor of Virginia, in his speech the other day, exclaimed, "Give me Jew or Gentile, dog or devil, I care not which, so we beat Grant."

Yes, anything to beat Gen. Grant; traduce him, vilify him, put him out of the way. They know full well that while Gen. Grant is at the head, the amendments to the Constitution and the Reconstruction laws will be respected. With keenest instinct, they preceive that Grant, with his dogged obstinacy, his iron will and his immovable courage, is the deadliest foe to any violation of the nation's rights as settled by the war.

Are these rights in any danger by the election of the secession candidate?

Let us see. The foremost of the Greeley men, the late Democratic candidate for Vice-President, the present Senator from Missouri, the fearless, outspoken Frank Blair, who scorns to conceal his real sentiments, declares that he stands by his Roadhead letter, which says:

"We must have a President who will execute the will of the people *by trampling into dust* the usurpations of Congress known as the Reconstruction acts."

And the *Caucasian*, a journal of Blair's own State, gives its platform thus:

"State sovereignty, *white supremacy*, and REPUDIATION! This is liberty!

"Our platform : *The Constitution of* 1860, and the rights of the States!

"DOWN WITH THE FIFTEENTH AMENDMENT!

"Direct taxation and the rightful representation of all the States, or ANOTHER REBELLION!"

On the 26th of May last, Jefferson Davis, addressing the people of Georgia, at Augusta, said :

"It is not a tribute to me individually, but *because you feel that I am one of yourselves that you come to do me honor.* You *know me only as the representative of your cause. That cause is dear to me—more precious even than life* [applause], *and I glory in its remembrance.* My simplest words may work you harm. If I say, 'Good night, my friends, go to your homes,' and a Congressional investigating committee happened to be within hearing, its members would swear that I directed you to go off and join the *Ku-Kiux.* [Laughter and applause.] *Filled with that jealousy which springs from the knowledge of their inferiority, and of the justice of your pretensions*, and conscious of broken covenants and a violated constitution, they mistrust every movement, and tremble with fear when they think that right may again prevail."

Two days later he addressed the people of Atlanta as follows :

"I am not of those who accept the situation. I accept nothing."

"These cant phrases that we hear so much about of 'accepting the situation,' and about our rights having been submitted to the 'arbitrament of the sword,' are but the excuses of cowards. And, then, my friends, about the much talked of subject of 'accepting the situation.' You are not called upon to acknowledge that you have done wrong unless you feel it. I don't believe I did any wrong, and, therefore, I don't acknowledge it. Wait patiently until the tide turns—as sooner or later turn it will—and the day is not far distant when the sun will shine upon you a free, independent and sovereign State."

With utterances like this the Southern journals literally abound.

But we have fresher expressions upon this subject. I read from the *World's* reports of Mr. Greeley's speech made at Pittsburg, last Thursday. He says :

"I was one of those who said, 'No, there is no such alternative; I deny that the Southern people, the great majority of them, are against the Union. I demand that there shall be a fair, open, free discussion before all that Southern people, of an honest, unterrified, unconstrained vote, and if they approve, if the people of the South say they want disunion, I will consent to it. [Cheers.] I know they will not.' I knew that the Southern people, that the great majority, must have voted as they actually did that winter, not for secession but for clinging to the Union. [Cheers.] And now, to-day, if the nation was to be imperilled, and there were just two modes of saving it—to trust to the chances of civil war, or to the chances of a free vote of the Southern people – I would very greatly prefer to take the latter chance rather than the former."

A few days before this speech was made there was a convention of the soldiers and sailors of the war at Pittsburg. In the *Evening Post* and *New York Times* of the 16th inst. you will find the following:

"BALTIMORE, Sept. 15.—The rebellious spirit which animated the people of this city during the late war, and which was exhibited in positive acts of violence whenever they could be indulged in with impunity, was shown this evening to be as strong as ever. The Washington veterans, in passing through the city on the way to Pittsburg to the Soldiers' and Sailors' Convention, were attacked, at 7 o'clock, by ruffians concealed behind railway cars, at the Calvert street depot.

"The scenes of 1861 were repeated in their main features, and one soldier was seriously injured, having been struck by a brick, which smashed his face in a shocking manner."

The Massachusetts Sixth met with the same reception in 1861.

Mr. Greeley says "let us shake hands over the bloody bodies." "It is all wrong for the *North* to keep up these feelings."

In the same speech Mr. Greeley gives his views about the soldiers and sailors who convened at Pittsburg, thus:

"The party that meets here and shouts for Grant and Wilson: No other party requires that any human being should stand proscribed on our soil for a rebellion that ceased seven and a half years ago. No party, no man of any party but this, *the very party that held a great military parade* this week in order to further separate and divide the hearts of the American people from each other. [Cheers.] They hold essential to their triumph that hatred should continue; that distress, suspicion, and alienation should continue. Do what you will, do what you may, they are determined not to be satisfied."

How unreasonable these northern soldiers are, not "*to be satisfied*" with being murdered on their way to save the capital from traitors, and with having their "faces smashed in" on their way to meet their brave comrades who had survived the war.

Mr. Greeley says these men are all of the "Grant and Wilson Party;" so they are; and if he will take an elevation where he can look over into the 5th of November next, he will see an interminable throng—some with armless sleeves, some with artificial legs, some pale from the sufferings of the war, leaning on their old fathers for support, some with the port of health and military mien, some with the sailor's swing—all moving on, with no arms in their hands, but little paper billets in their stead. That, Mr. Greeley, is what you called at Pittsburg "the military parade, the Grant and Wilson Party." Including their kindred and their grateful countrymen, a formidable array! You are right, they are for Grant and Wilson; *shame* sits forever upon the *soldier* who votes for Horace Greeley!

Why did the Democratic Party nominate Mr. Greeley? On what bargain was it done? Just before this unnatural alliance was made public, the *World*, the ablest journal in the Democratic ranks, said: Mr. Greeley's sole hope of an election depends upon his receiving the unanimous support of the Democratic Party. * * * If he is nominated by the Democratic Convention and elected by Democratic votes, he cannot ignore the Democratc Party in organizing his administration. * * * If Democratis are to vote for Mr. Greeley, it must be *under such circumstances* that he will be *compelled* to acknowledge his obligations to the party, and will *make* him *dependent* on it for the success of his administration." The *circumstances* were all arranged to mutual satisfaction, and Horace Greeley received the unanimous nomination of that party which he had lately pronounced so utterly disloyal and rebel at the core.

We know where we stand. We have two great parties in the field: The old Bourbon Democratic Party, with its ancient bigotries, it secession sympathies, its rebel supporters; "with the hate, the chagrin, the wrath, the mortification of ten bitter years to impel and guide its steps." On the other hand, we have the Republican Party; with no hate or chagrin or wrath, but with a record of more than ten years of patriotic devotion and glorious deeds of imperishable renown.

Past experience proves that the Southern politicians never mistook their man; they never accepted a Northern President unless sure of his Southern principles, and they have not changed; they do no even pretend to have changed; they boldly say that the advocate of secession and the bailer of Jeff. Davis is reliable, and that he will surely see that they are paid for their liberated slaves—the four hundred million which he once proposed. Everywhere throughout the South, you shall hear that they expect to be paid for their human chattels, if Mr. Greeley is elected. Let us see what Gov. Aiken, the great slave-holder of South Carolina, said upon this subject. I read from the speech of Senator Morton, delivered in this hall a few months since: "I met a very distinguished Southern gentlemen at West Point, last summer—a man that you all know by reputation; and I will give you his name, because it was not said in confidence to me, but was said in the presence of others; one of the noblest and purest men of the South, and a loyal man throughout the war, and of the largest slave-holders throughout the South—Gov. Aiken, of South Carolina. He believed slavery to have been unlawfully abolished, and he said: 'I have made out an inventory of my slaves and laid it aside, because I believe that a sense of returning justice will yet compel this nation to pay for the slaves.' And so far as I know, this has been done by almost the entire body of the former slave-owners of the Southern States. When the Democratic party comes into power, they will come forward with that claim, and they will say to the Democracy, and say truly: 'You are committed in favor of paying us for our slaves.'"

But some one says that the Fourteenth Amendment to the Constitution forbids such payment. So it does; but the Fourteenth Amendment will go where the Missouri Compromise went, and be "*trampled in the dust*" with the other reconstruction measures, if Mr. Greeley is elected.

You will then see troubled times in our financial affairs, and general distrust. Four hundred million is a large corruption fund, and the Fourteenth Amendment would be as a spider's web. Remember the Missouri Compromise.

Gen. Grant or Horace Greeley in the Presidency! A momentous trust! A nation's prosperity hangs upon this issue. We have tried Gen. Grant; Mr. Greeley we have not tried. Grant holds aloft the Republican banner—its inscriptions you have all read.

Greeley holds up the Democratic standard; to it is tied the rebel flag—yes, and Horace Greeley bears it! and if elected, its folds will cover over his face, and blind his eyes, and his masters, hating and despising him, will tie him with fetters of brass, and take him down to Washington, and make him grind in their prison-house. He cannot help it. Even the strongest man is not so strong as the party which elects him.

Senator Sumner says in his letter: "Horace Greeley stood forth a Reformer and Abolitionist; President Grant enlisted as a Pro-slavery Democrat, and at the election of Buchanan, fortified by his vote all the pretensions of slavery."

Well, what if we concede all that? Is Gen. Grant now the less an earnest Republican? If Judas, an original disciple, had reproached St. Paul with having been once a persecutor of the Church, that would not have helped Judas or hurt St. Paul.

There happens to be another man on your ticket whom Mr. Sumner would call a pro-slavery Democrat, voting for Buchanan. He not only voted for Buchanan, but was in Buchanan's Cabinet. He is the same man who, while there as Secretary of the Treasury, gave the memorable order: "If any man attempts to haul down the American flag, shoot him on the spot."

Don't you think the old flag will be safe in the hands of Gen. Dix? And when he is Governor, do you think the thieves will dare break into the public treasury and steal?

Gen. Dix has held some place of trust from the time he was eighteen years old. He has discharged the duties of all these offices with ability, fidelity, untarnished and unsuspected virtue.

Your city, your county and your State have long been plundered. Even your Reform Legislature could not alone protect us, and the people call Gen. Dix to the rescue. And here the tried old faithful veteran comes. The people know that they can trust *him*, and the great swelling wave will lift this honest man to the highest office in the State—the last, just, crowning reward of an honest life.

But there was another "Pro-slavery Democrat" in Mr. Buchanan's Cabinet, who, when he found that slave-holders were enemies of the Union, turned like a lion in his lair, and with energy unparalleled, with indignation unmatched, and with a directness and devotion which could not be surpassed, took the side of liberty, and by night and by day, gave his great mind, and his very life, in its noblest prime, to save his country; and when the lightning wires told that Edwin M. Stanton had been called to his great reward, did Charles Sumner reproachfully say: "He was a Pro-slavery Democrat, and in the election of Buchanan fortified, by his vote, all the pretensions of slavery."

Mr. Sumner also delivered an elaborate oration in the Senate of the United States, with intent to degrade the President in the eyes of the civilized world; carefully revised and printed before it was pronounced; part of the material used was a dead man's words, claimed to have been whispered in the confidence-chamber of the dying Secretary. I forbear considering at length the propriety of ever repeating such conversations for any purpose, and especially for the purpose of defaming the Chief Magistrate of your country, with whom you have disagreed. But I cannot waive considering the probable truth of the statement which Mr. Sumner makes.

He says that Mr. Stanton, just before he died, told him this:

"'I know General Grant better than any other person in the country can know him. It was my duty to study him, and I did so night and day—when I saw him and when I did not see him—and now I tell you what I know: he cannot govern this country.' The intensity of his manner and the positiveness of his judgment surprised me; for though I was aware that the late Secretary of War did not place the President very high in general capacity, I was not prepared for a judgment so strongly couched. At last, after some delay, occupied in meditating his remarkable words, I observed, 'What you say is very broad.' 'It is as true as it is broad,' he replied promptly. I added, 'You are tardy; you tell this late; why did you not say it before his nomination?' He answered that he was not consulted about the nomination, and had no opportunity of expressing his opinion upon it, besides being much occupied at the time by his duties as Secretary of War and his contest with the President. I followed by saying, 'But you took part in the Presidential election, and made a succession of speeches for him in Ohio and Pennsylvania.' 'I spoke,' said he, 'but I never introduced the name of Gen. Grant. I spoke for the Republican Party and the Republican cause.' This was the last time I saw Mr. Stanton. A few days later I followed him to the grave where he now rests."

I have before me the speeches to which Mr. Sumner alludes, and I find the name of Gen. Grant mentioned twenty-one times in a single speech, and in each of them that name is spoken with the greatest respect. In his speech at Philadelphia occurs the following;

"In Grant we behold the leader of our armies in the path of victory. In Grant we behold the great General, who, under Divine Providence, led our armies, supported, as they were, by some of these who are before you to-night. * * * *

"The mistakes mentioned are, Seymour says, 'the mistakes of the Republican Party.'" What, then, has Gen. Grant got to do with them? [Cheers for Grant.] While Congress may have made mistakes, if you please, without number—day by day made mistakes—Grant was before the enemy's face fighting him; he was taking no surrender, except that it was 'Unconditional!' No terms left his lips but 'Unconditional surrender' of the enemy of his country."

I might detain you long with extracts of similar tone; but these suffice to show how inaccurate was Mr. Sumner where absolute verity was so easy to be obtained. The other part of the statement depends upon Mr. Sumner's memory of words from lips which speak no more; that kind of evidence, in courts of justice, is received with exceeding caution, and, if inconsistent with established facts, it is not believed at all.

It is known to some of you that for many years I was very intimate with the great Secretary, and was one of the friends who bore him to his grave. I saw him often during his last illness, and have a large number of letters from him, several of which relate to Gen. Grant, and one to Gen. Dix; their testimony will be more convincing than uncertain words repeated long after their alleged utterance, and by one whose mind and imagination had grown morbid and diseased by brooding over grievances of a personal kind.

His letter about Gen. Dix, alike honorable to Mr. Stanton and just to Gen. Dix, I will read first:

WASHINGTON, April 16, 1862.

Hon. EDWARDS PIERREPONT:

My Dear Sir—This morning my son called my attention to a paragraph in the New York *Ledger* of Saturday, April 5, on page 4, ascribing to me the authorship of Gen. Dix's telegram to New Orleans, and saying that it has high authority that I wrote it. Will you be so good as to call on Mr. Bonner and inform him, from me, that I did *not* write that order, that its author was Gen. Dix, and request him to correct the *Ledger's* mistake, in order that credit may be given to whom it justly belongs.

The correction might be made in some such way as the following: "We are requested to state, on the authority of Mr. Stanton, that the famous telegram sent by Gen. Dix to a naval officer in New Orleans in these words—'*The first man that attempts to haul down the American flag, shoot him on the spot!*'—was written by Gen. Dix—that the credit of that order belongs to Gen. Dix, and not to Mr. Stanton."

You may perhaps suppose the correction of this mistake is a small matter, and not worthy of attention in times like these.

But that order was a historic fact of much significance in a very dark hour. I admired it at the time it was made; would be proud of it if it belonged to me; and desire to see its merit acknowledged and awarded to him who alone is entitled to it—Gen. Dix. How it could ever be ascribed to me I cannot conceive, and would be glad if you would ask Mr. Bonner upon whose authority the statement was made, in order that the erroneous impression may be corrected to its fullest extent.

Yours truly,
EDWIN M. STANTON.

Soon after the November election, he wrote as follows:

WASHINGTON, Nov. 13, 1868.

HON. EDWARDS PIERREPONT :

My Dear Sir—Your letter reached me here on my return home from Baltimore, where I had been making a visit for rest and change of air. For your kind appreciation of my political exertions, made under much debility and suffering, please accept my thanks. * * * During my absence, Gen. Grant returned home ; but, confined to my house, I have not seen him. Divine Providence seems to have furnished us with a fit President as well as a great General.

On the 1st of December, 1868, he wrote again, expressing the like confidence.

It will be remembered that the date of this conversation, as fixed by Mr. Sumner, was after the President had called in person upon Mr. Stanton, and tendered him the office of Judge of the Supreme Court, which Mr. Stanton accepted, and about which he had often spoken in warm eulogy of Gen. Grant. May we not safely conclude that Mr. Sumner's wearied brain needs rest?

We will consider the fitness of Gen. Grant and Horace Greeley for the great office. I know them both pretty well ; I shall try to present them to you fairly. Remember that it is the chief ruler of a great people, after a great civil war, whom you are about to select. The abilities which we seek are those of a great governor ; not those of an artist, a poet or man of letters ; men of science, writers, orators and literary men, from Cicero to Lamartine, have always failed as rulers of the State. No man of sense believes that Juvenal, Raphael, Shakespeare, Milton, Newton or La Place could ever have governed the nations whose history they adorned ; whereas, Julius Cæsar, Charlemagne, Frederick the Great, Napoleon, William of Orange, and more than all, the great Cromwell, were able rulers, each of whom was first a great soldier, and then a statesman of imperishable fame. Come down in history to our own country. Our first great ruler was the immortal Washington, the great Captain of his age.

The next marked ruler was Gen. Jackson, whose military fame preceded his civil reputation. The greatest rulers in every age have been the greatest soldiers of their time. Painters, sculptors, scholars, writers and journalists of other men's deeds, have always failed at the helm of State. They have not that combination of faculties and of will which the position requires. Upon this subject the instincts of mankind have generally guided them aright. Horace Greeley is a man of eminent abilities, but as unsuited to the Presidential office as was the poet Horace for an Emperor of Rome. It is one of the weaknesses of our people, to imagine for the moment, that the man who has achieved great success in anything, is fitted for the Presidency; and hence we have had successful steamboat men, express men, railroad men, telegraph men, explorers, pathfinders, writers and journalists talked of as candidates for the chief executive office.

Rosa Bonheur can paint a horse better than any living artist, but she can't shoe one.

I would not detract from Mr. Greeley's justly-earned reputation—he has immense industry and a powerful pen which he has always used on the side of humanity. He is a true hater of oppression and of privileged class—very placable and of kindly nature. In money matters, honest; in politics, more far-sighted than is generally supposed, and shrewd even to cunning; with large love of approbation, the spring of his great ambition. Able as a journalist, vigorous as a writer, and always in sympathy with liberal principals; he never keeps an even course, and often startles his friends by crotchets the more dangerous because sincere. He is liable to influences of whose evil he is not conscious. His best friends would never select him to lead an army, to preside over a turbulent assembly, to control a bank or run a railroad. He has never shown any of the qualities of a great leader, and we have no right to suppose that he can now make an able ruler over a great nation. A noted letter, which Mr. Greeley has been careful to republish, written to Gov. Seward when he quarreled with the Governor and Thurlow Weed, will throw light upon the temper, the ambition and real character of this Liberal candidate for the Presidency. We read from it as follows:

"You were Governor, dispensing patronage worth $3,000 to $20,000 per year to your friends and compatriots, and I returned to my garret and my crust. I believe it did not then occur to me that *some one of these abundant places might have been offered to me without injustice;* I now think it should have occurred to *you.*

* * * * * *

"In the Harrison campaign of 1840, I was again designated to edit a campaign paper. I published it as well, and ought to have made something by it, in spite of its extremely low price; my extreme poverty was the main reason why I did not. *

"Now came the great scramble of the swell-mob of coon-minstrels and cider-suckers at Washington—*I not being counted in.* Several regiments of them went on from this City, but no one of the whole crowd—though I say it, who should not—had done so much toward Gen. Harrison's nomination and election as yours respectfully. I asked nothing, expected nothing; *but you, Gov. Seward, ought to have asked that I be Postmaster of New York.*" * * * *

"But this last Spring, after the Nebraska question had created a new state of things at the North, one or two personal friends, of no political consideration, suggested my name as a candidate for Governor, and I did not discourage them. * * *

"I suspect it is true that I could not have been elected Governor as a Whig. But had he and you been favorable, there *would* have been a party in the State, ere this, which could and would have elected me to any post, without injuring myself or endangering your re-election. * * * *

"I should have hated to serve as Lieutenant-Governor, but I should have gloried in running for the post. I want to have my enemies all upon me at once—I am tired of fighting them piecemeal. And, although I should have been beaten in the canvass, I know that my running would have helped the ticket and HELPED MY PAPER." * * * *

Are these the breathings of a lofty patriotism, or do you distinguish the vengeful odor of a bitterly disappointed personal ambition?

When Richard, the usurping king, asked his trusted page whom he could call to aid in his most wicked and ambitious scheme against the safety of the State, the page replied: "I know a discontented gentleman, whose humble means match not his haughty mind."

Gen. Grant, for the public, never talks or writes or speaks; he is inarticulate—silent. He does not impress men generally. He seems inert, and in mixed society draws into his shell. To this nation of ceaseless talkers he seems a kind of Sphynx. But he has *done* some things. He is younger than Horace Greeley by more than eleven years; he has done things for this people which Horace Greeley could not do—which no other man could do.

The danger is over now, and almost forgot; but there was a time, a gloomy time, when this nation's life was in peril; when ten thousand Horace Greelyes could not save it, and Gen. Grant did. We tried many other Generals, all well placed in the social scale, supported by all the upper influences in the land; all failed. An obscure man from Galena, poor, of no reputation or family influence, led the Union armies from victory to victory, and *never failed*; and when the sword of Lee was surrenderd to his younger victor, the nation offered up heartfelt thanksgivings to God, and Grant was almost worshiped as the savior of our liberties! Are you going to *crucify* him now? Why, what evil hath he done? My brave and honest countrymen, you do not mean to be unjust. Gen. Grant don't seek this office. He never did seek it. He don't want to be driven from it in disgrace by the enemies of the country which his brave comrades died to save. Let us look over the record of the past four years, and see what evil he hath done. You called this soldier, forty-six years old, to take the helm of State in the perplexing troubled days which followed a great civil war. Four millions of ignorant slaves had been freed, a powerful confederation of States in war had been subdued by arms. Wholly unused to public affairs and to political tricks, this inexperienced man was placed in the Presidential chair. Did you deem him so far from human that he could make no blunders? and is that his crime that you thought him so perfect that you pardon no mistake? I read his modest words in accepting the re-nomination:

"If elected in November, and protected by a kind Providence in health and strength to perform the duties of the high trust conferred, I promise the same zeal and devotion to the good of the whole people for the future of my official life as shown in the past. Past experience may guide me in avoiding mistakes inevitable with novices in all professions and in all occupations."

Modest, as he is always modest. I have known him since long before the surrender of Lee, and never did I hear him tell of any of his victories; never heard him even allude to them;

never heard him utter a word that would indicate that he had achieved anything. Who ever heard of a boast or vain word from his quiet lips? All who know him will bear witness to the same unpretentious, simple ways of this remarkable man.

Can you tell me why this great effort to drive him from the office which he has so worthily filled? I think I can tell.

General Grant had proved himself so great a man that the nation expected too much—more than was reasonable; they expected *perfection*, and would tolerate nothing less in their idol: and, true to our English blood, we began to think that he had been overpraised—a crime which the Anglo-Saxon race never allows to go unpunished. In a republic, where office is open to all, each office had a thousand aspirants. Each office filled made many enemies and sometimes an ingrate. The vanity and pretension of official aspirants is amazing. Grant had no skill to flatter, and no wish to excite false hopes. When all the offices were filled the disappointed became sour, and talked about patriotism, and hinted at the incapacity and possible corruption of the Executive. Many concealed their grief, hoping that something might turn up, until the Presidential term was drawing to its close, and the time came for new combinations through which new hopes were excited in the thousands of expectants for place; and in looking about they saw better chances in a new deal, and hence the noisy *outs*, vastly outnumbering the quiet *ins*, got up a din to drown every voice which tried to speak in refutation of the foul slanders with which the President was assailed. Many were restless and wanted a change for the sake of change, thinking little of what a change might involve. Some honest people were made to believe that the President was growing rich, while every well-informed person knew that his income did not meet his necessary expenses. Jealousy of his position; jealousy which plays so vile a part in public affairs, came in, and vague distrust, fomented by envy and disappointment, and rebel hate of him who crushed their treason, all joined in general plan to oust the President from his seat, and out of the grand jumble came a result, unexpected, unwished, and which amazed every leader of the movement, and for a time paralyzed their action. They had sown the wind, they did not expect the whirlwind would force Horace Greely upon them; and when the clouds cleared away and they saw that ghost appear, they stared aghast, like the murderous Thane at the ghost of Banquo!

The great God has his own mysterious way to bring about results; through fiery trials He sends all men destined for exalted deeds. Grant is as sure to be the next President as is the continued motion of the planetary spheres, and the terrible ordeal through which he is to pass presages great events in the next five years. When the people have seen him walk through the fires and come out with his mantle unsinged they will reproach themselves for the cruelties which they have allowed him to suffer; but he will be purified and strengthened for the great work which lies before him.

Alex. H. Stephens, by far the most philosophic and appreciative intellect in the Southern States, has recorded, in an elaborate history of the war, his opinion of General Grant. Mr. Stephens says:

"I was instantly struck with the great simplicity and perfect naturalness of his manners, and the entire absence of everything like affectation, show, or even the usual military air or mien of men in his position. He was plainly attired, sitting in a log-cabin, busily writing on a small table by a kerosene-lamp. It was night when we arrived. There was nothing in his appearance or surroundings which indicated his official rank. There were neither guards nor aids about him. Upon Colonel Babcock's rapping at his door, the response 'Come in' was given by himself in a tone of voice and with a cadence which I can never forget.

"His conversation was easy and fluent, without the least effort or restraint. In this nothing was so closely noticed by me as the point and terseness with which he expressed whatever he said. He did not seem either to court or avoid conversation, but, whenever he did speak, what he said was to the point, and covered the whole matter in a few words. I saw before being with him long that he was exceedingly quick in perception and direct in purpose, with a vast deal more of brains than tongue, as ready as that was at his command.

"We were here with General Grant two days. * * * He furnished us with comfortable quarters on board one of his dispatch-boats. The more I became acquainted with him the more I became thoroughly impressed with the very extraordinary combination of rare elements of character which he exhibited. During the time he met us frequently and conversed freely upon various subjects, not much upon our mission. I saw, however, very clearly, that he was very anxious for the proposed conference to take place, and, from all that was said, I inferred—whether correctly or not I do not know—that he was fully apprised of its proposed object.

"Upon the whole, the result of this first acquaintance with General Grant, beginning with our going to and ending with our return from Hampton Roads, was the conviction on my mind that, taken all in all, he was one of the most remarkable men I had ever met with, and that his career in life, if his days should be prolonged, was hardly entered upon; that his character was not yet fully developed; that he himself was not aware of his own power, and that, if he lived, he would in the future exert a controlling influence in shaping the destinies of this country, either for good or evil. Which it would be, time and circumstances alone could disclose. That was the opinion of him then formed, and it is the same which has been uniformly expressed by me ever since."

The career of Grant has been a marvel from the beginning—not to be explained upon the ordinary principles of judging men. With reverent voice, I say that I believe he is raised up by Providence for greater deeds than he has yet performed. I find nothing in history which he resembles except the great Cromwell, and I find no such self-poised head as his since Cromwell died. I am an earnest advocate for the re-election of Gen. Grant because I believe in him—because I think it, under the circumstances, the only safety for the country. I am not an office-holder, and, as we are talking rather confidentially to-night, I will tell you that I do not intend to be. I have taken the full measure of that matter. I intend to remain your fellow-citizen with unsealed lips, free to criticize any man who holds the people's trust and to denounce any man who betrays it.

I have given some study to the system of our government, and tried to learn the source of its power and its real dangers. It differs radically from all others. No feudal seed was ever planted in our soil, and the feeble attempts to engraft feudal scions on our stock failed, as they will always fail. No reverence for great families or historic names has any hold here. In theory and in fact the power lies down in the hearts of the people, and their will gets expressed through public opinion, from which there is no appeal. Office, being open to all, until within a few years, was generally sought for. the advancement of social position, to gratify personal pride and love of eminent consideration for public service, or to perform a useful duty to the State. As wealth increased and corrupting luxury came in, bad, cunning men discovered that they could use official trusts to steal the earnings of the people under the cover of deceiving laws; and the cheated citizens were made to believe that the fraudulent taxes all came out of the rich; though they were puzzled to see how it was that the rich grew richer and the poor poorer, while no taxes were levied upon the poor. They are just now beginning to learn that all taxes really come out of the labor and industry of the people, and that the idea that capital pays the taxes is a covert fraud—the great cost of rent which the laboring poor and the industrious mechanic or clerk has to pay is chiefly caused by the fraudulent tax which the tenement pays.

No honest men but the rich can ever grow rich in a government where your officials are robbers and levy taxes for plunder. If we cannot preserve our government from official corruption our liberties are near their end. Come up and face this question, fellow-citizens; do you believe that the election of Horace Greeley will work reform? Do you not know that his election will throw a pall over every cheerful hope of rescuing our city and State from robbers? Do you not know that the thieves will run under his skirts for shelter, and tell him that they are sorry, and "eager to clasp hands across the bloody chasm," and only want to be let alone, until they can work back through plausible device into their former places.

Reformers, you know very well that the election of Horace Greeley does not mean reform. You cannot face an honest audience and tell them that you think so. If you do they will not believe you. A desire for reform swept this State like a whirlwind last Autumn, and it will do it again. I know that we shall have reform or despotism. I do not believe that the election of Horace Greeley tends to reform, but to confusion and anarchy; and you all know what follows anarchy. I shall do what I can to elect Gen. Grant, and then I shall do what I can to aid in placing able and honest men around him, and if he proves recreant to his trust and corrupted by continued power, uses his great office for unholy purposes, I will be free and as earnest and as public in denunciation as I am now in my advocacy. I have chosen my path in life, and I intend to walk in it, fearless of thieves and scoundrels, and bad men in high places. Life has no value without liberty, and where you dare not speak the truth, there is no liberty.

Mr. Greeley very fairly said that Gen. Grant had made a better President than he had expected, and that he would do better the second time than the first. I shall not be found abusing Mr. Greeley; I venerate the much good he has done; in a few short weeks no living man will excite so much of our condolence. The dishonest men who have been deluding him, cheating him, will desert him, revile him, and with lusty oaths declare that they never knew him; swear that it was all a joke, that they never expected to elect him, and that the whole fantastic trick was a juggling fraud. The discussion of this question, and the universal intelligence circulated through the priceless services of the Press, have awakened the people. They begin to see how unjustly the President has been slandered, how difficult has been his task, and how well, upon the whole, he has performed it. Men of business, men of substance, men of families whom you love, come face to face with this question, and you will shudder at the peril which you have escaped. I know that you will not support this nomination, conceived in fraud, against the peace and prosperity of your country. You will vote for Gen. Grant, and thank God that the good sense of the people tells them how wiser it is to "let well enough alone," "to bear the little ills we have than fly to others that we know not of." Security, confidence, development and unexampled prosperity will surely follow the election of Grant.

No one who has had opportunity can fail to notice how carefully the bankers, merchants and business men of other countries watch our political action. They care nothing for our candidates, but only regard the matter as affecting our credit and the safety of our bonds. Men of business in Europe cannot believe it possible that a sober nation like ours is going to upset its policy, radically change its Administration—disturb all, just as it is beginning to be settled, and thus discredit and drive back our securities, stop all negotiations, and put an end to the vast enterprises now starting to develop and enrich our country. The answer to these apprehensions is: *The people are not going to do it.* Every man I meet, Democrat or Republican, makes some halting excuse when he says that he is for Greeley—talks about "the lesser of two evils," "the surroundings of Grant" and other apologetic trifles, showing that his heart is not in it, and that his conscience revolts at this violence to common sense. When the time comes to count the vote, the party will be amazed at the feeble show, and awake to the fact that a straight-out Democrat would have polled a *much larger vote.* And the sagacious *World* will point to its issues of last spring and justly say: "*I told you so.*"

A word about Gen. Grant's oppression of the South, and I have done. Last February I went through most of the Southern States and tried to learn their real condition. They were not very prosperous—they were nearly all for Greeley, even then; I mean the rebel whites, not the loyal blacks. Since the war the South has suffered a good deal from bad government—no doubt of that—but much of it was incident to the situation, and more was due to their own sullen pride and obstinate will. Had they frankly accepted the inevitable, and returned to their allegiance, and honestly tried to aid the Government in reconstruction, they would have suffered little from misrule; the victorious North would have been over-generous to the fallen foe, and would have readily removed every disability. I sincerely believe that, before another year has passed, the South itself will rejoice in the re-election of Gen. Grant. And now, when we are at peace with all the world, when our prosperity is great and our industries are fast reviving, we are asked to make a change, to try something new, "to clasp our eager hands across the bloody chasm" (the South has shown no haste to shake hands). Govern justly, generously; protect the freedman in his rights; but do not, in blind fatuity, surrender the very ark of your liberties to those, who in peace, were so faithless, who in war could perpetrate or permit the inhuman cruelties of Andersonville and the Libby.

www.ingramcontent.com/pod-product-compliance
Lightning Source LLC
LaVergne TN
LVHW012329100826
845148LV00017B/677